High Protein

Vegan

Cookbook

Disclaimer

About the Book

If you are on the lookout for a comprehensive diet that helps you tone your body and enhance your overall health, then look no further than a protein-rich vegan diet! The diet has been designed to help people lose weight and also build lean muscles that do not burn away easily. The protein-rich diet is quite easy to adopt and can be transitioned into without much hassle.

The biggest question on people's minds when they hear of the vegan diet is *Where do I get my protein intake from?* But the fact is that plant-based products have ample amounts of protein, and if you cook your food with the right ingredients, plant-based protein will provide you with more than enough to build a lean body.

This book is designed so that you can follow a protein-rich vegan diet without having to struggle to search for new recipes. The recipes in this book are easy to cook, 100% vegan, and rich in protein. Novice and expert cooks will enjoy these recipes and make use of all the best vegan ingredients that one can buy from the market.

Once you are done reading this book, you will want to rush to the kitchen and begin work on your vegan menu. So, without further ado, let's get started!

About the Author

Sam Kuma is passionate about sharing his culinary experience to the world. His work involves modernization of healthy diet plans. He has published many recipe books for vegan, ketogenic, and paleo diets, dash food cooking, and several cookbooks on ethnic cuisines. His main focus is to make healthy diets like vegan and ketogenic mainstream by sharing easy-to-create, appetizing recipes. In his first two books regarding vegan recipes, he has produced delicious vegan chocolates, desserts, ice creams, burgers, and sandwiches.

Table of Contents

Introduction

The vegan diet is easily one of the healthiest diets in the world and for good reason. Not only does it help in cutting down on the existing fat in your body but it also enhances your disease fighting capacity. It is designed to provide people with a complete solution to their weight loss issues and aid them in slimming down.

A vegan diet refers to a plant-based diet where meat and animal products are completely eliminated. It also promotes the consumption of animal-derived products such as eggs, dairy, and honey. Vegans are often described as ethical vegetarians, as they do not consume any animal-related products.

Proteins make for one of the most important nutrients in the body and are chiefly responsible for building up muscles. The best way to build lean muscles is by first tearing the old ones through exercise and then forcing them to heal into leaner ones. This is only possible if you bombard your body with high doses of proteins, which is exactly what the protein-rich vegan diet is designed to do.

The diet incorporates the use of protein-rich foods such as chickpeas, quinoa, soya and rice bran, which help in building lean muscles. The diet is extremely nutritious and will eliminate the need for supplements. However, you might have to consult a physician before taking it up to ensure that you do not need any calcium supplements.

The recipes in this book are simple to make and will inspire you to keep going. But you need not limit yourself to just these ideas. Feel free to come up with some recipes of your own. As long as you make use of the core ingredients, you can experiment to your heart's content!

Let's begin!

Chapter 1: High Protein Vegan Smoothie Recipes

Banana Almond Cream Shake

Prep: 5 min	Total: 7 min	Servings: 2

Ingredients:

- 1 scoop rice protein
- 1 scoop pea protein
- 2 bananas, peeled, chopped
- 1 1/2 cups almond milk or soy milk
- 30 almonds

Instructions:

1. Blend together all the ingredients in a blender until smooth.

2. Serve in tall glasses with crushed ice.

Kale 'n Berry Smoothie

Prep: 10 min	Total: 12 min	Servings: 2

Ingredients:

- 1 cup kale leaves, discard hard stems and ribs, torn

- 2/3 cup strawberries, chopped

- 2/3 cup blueberries

- 2 medium bananas, peeled, sliced

- 1 cup almond milk

- 2 tablespoons chia seeds + extra for serving

- 2 tablespoons hemp powder

- 2 tablespoons ground flax seeds

- 2 tablespoons acai berry

- 2 teaspoons ground cinnamon

Instructions:

1. Place all the ingredients in a blender and blend until smooth.

2. Pour into tall glasses.

3. Sprinkle chia seeds on top. Serve with crushed ice.

Salted Chocolate Oatmeal Smoothie

Prep: 3 min	Total: 5 min	Servings: 4

Ingredients:

- 2 cups soy yogurt
- 2 ripe bananas, peeled, sliced
- 4 tablespoons cocoa powder
- 2 cups water
- 4 scoops vegan plant-based chocolate protein powder
- 2 teaspoons vanilla
- 1/2 teaspoon salt
- 1 cup old fashioned oats or quick cooking oats

Instructions:

1. Place all the ingredients in a blender and blend until smooth.

2. Pour into tall glasses.

3. Serve with crushed ice.

Nuts n Seeds Smoothie

Prep: 10 min	Total: 12 min	Servings: 2

Ingredients:

- 1 tablespoons hemp seeds

- 15 almonds, chopped

- 1 cup fresh cherries, pitted

- 11/2 cups almond milk

-

Instructions:

1. Place all the ingredients in a blender and blend until smooth.

2. Pour into a tall glass. Serve with crushed ice.

Smoothie in a Bowl

Prep: 5 min	Total: 7 min	Servings: 4

Ingredients:

For Smoothie:

- 1 cup blueberries
- 1 1/2 cups raspberries
- 2 large bananas, peeled, sliced, frozen
- 2 teaspoons acai berry powder
- 2 cups water
- 4 scoops vanilla pea protein powder
- 2 teaspoons chia seeds

For topping:

- 1 cup blueberries

- 1/2 cup blackberries

- 1/2 cup raspberries

- 2 large bananas, sliced

- 10 walnuts, chopped

Instructions:

1. Place all the ingredients of the smoothie in a blender and blend until smooth.

2. Pour into bowls.

3. Sprinkle the toppings and serve.

Chapter 2: High Protein Vegan Breakfast Recipes

Homemade Cereal

Prep: 5 min	Total: 5 min	Servings: 20-25

Ingredients:

- 1 1/2 cups chia seeds

- 1 1/2 cups buckwheat groats

- 1 1/2 cups hemp seeds

- 1/2 cup raisins

- 1/2 cup walnuts

- 1/2 cup almonds

- 1/2 cup chopped, dried apple

- 1/2 cup dried cranberries

22

- 2 teaspoons ground cinnamon

Instructions:

1. Mix together all the ingredients in a bowl. Transfer into an airtight container.

2. Store in a cool and dry place. Use as and when desired.

3. Serve with soymilk, almond milk, or hemp milk with fresh fruits.

Hey, are you enjoying the book? I'd love to hear your thoughts!

Many readers do not know how hard reviews are to come by, and how much they help an author.

I would be incredibly thankful if you could take just 60 seconds to write a brief review on Amazon, even if it's just a few sentences!

Please head to the product page, and leave a review as shown below.

Thank you for taking the time to share your thoughts!

Your review will genuinely make a difference for me and help gain exposure for my work.

Peanut Butter Granola

Prep: 5 min	Total: 20 min	Servings: 4-6

Ingredients:

- 2 cups oats

- 4 tablespoons maple syrup

- 4 tablespoons peanut butter

- 1/2 teaspoon vanilla extract

- 1/2 teaspoon ground cinnamon

Instructions:

1. Place maple syrup and peanut butter in a microwave-safe bowl. Microwave for 20-30 seconds.

2. Remove from the microwave and mix. Add cinnamon and vanilla and stir again.

3. Add oats and coat well. Transfer onto a greased baking sheet and spread it all over the baking sheet.

4. Bake in a preheated oven at 325° F for about 8-10 minutes or until light brown and crisp.

5. Cool completely and serve with the vegan milk of your choice.

French Toast

Prep: 10 min	Total: 15 min	Servings: 6

Ingredients:

- 2 medium ripe bananas, peeled, mashed

- 2 cups almond milk, unsweetened

- 1/2 teaspoon vanilla extract

- 12 slices vegan whole grain bread

- 1 teaspoon ground cinnamon

- 12 tablespoons maple syrup

- 6 strawberries, sliced

- 1 1/2 oranges, sliced

- 1 1/2 passion fruit, sliced

- 1 1/2 kiwis, peeled, sliced

28

- 1 1/2 cups grapes

- 14 cup nuts of your choice, chopped

- Cooking spray

Instructions:

1. Whisk together bananas, almond milk, cinnamon, and vanilla and set aside.

2. Place a nonstick skillet over medium heat. Spray cooking spray over it.

3. Gently dip a slice of bread in the banana mixture and immediately place on the heated skillet.

4. Cook until the underside is golden brown. Flip sides and cook the other side too.

5. Remove from skillet and serve with maple syrup and fruits and nuts.

6. Repeat steps 3, 4, and 5 with the remaining bread and serve.

Cinnamon Nut Quinoa

Prep: 5 min	Total: 20 min	Servings: 6

Ingredients:

- 1 1/2 cups quinoa, rinsed
- 1 1/2 cups water
- 1 1/2 cups almond milk
- 1 teaspoon ground cinnamon
- 3 cups fresh blueberries
- 1/2 cup almonds, chopped, toasted
- 3 tablespoons agave nectar

Instructions:

1. Place a saucepan over medium-high heat. Add water, milk, and quinoa and bring to the boil.
2. Lower heat, cover and simmer until almost dry.

3. Remove from heat and set aside for 5-7 minutes.

4. Fluff with a fork and divide into bowls.

5. Sprinkle blueberries and almonds. Add a teaspoon of agave

   nectar and serve.

6. If you find it too dry, pour some more almond milk and serve.

Vegan Frittata

Prep: 15 min	Total: 45-55 min	Servings: 8

Ingredients:

- 3 1/2 cups cooked brown rice

- 1 onion, chopped

- 8 cloves garlic, crushed, chopped

- 1 red bell pepper, chopped

- 1 yellow bell pepper, chopped

- 6 mushrooms, chopped

- 6 spring onions, chopped, keep the white and green parts separate

- 1 cup spinach, chopped

- 1 cup kale, chopped

- 2 egg replacers or 2 tablespoons flaxseed meal mixed with 4 tablespoons water

- 2 packages firm tofu

- 6 tablespoons nutritional yeast

- 1/2 cup fresh basil, chopped

- 4 teaspoons arrowroot

- 1 1/3 cups soy milk or almond milk

- 4 tablespoons soy sauce

- 2 tablespoons olive oil

- 4 teaspoons Dijon mustard

- Salt to taste

- 1 teaspoon turmeric

Instructions:

1. Mix rice and egg replacer together in a bowl and transfer the mixture into a large greased springform pan.

2. Press it well onto the bottom of the pan. Brush a little oil over it.

3. Bake in a preheated oven at 375° F for about 8-10 minutes. Remove from the oven and set aside.

4. Meanwhile, place a pan over medium heat. Add oil. When oil is heated, add onions, garlic, and whites of spring onion and sauté until translucent.

5. Add bell peppers and mushrooms and sauté for 3-4 minutes.

6. Add spinach, kale, basil and green part of spring onions. Sauté until all the greens wilts.

7. Lower heat.

8. Meanwhile, add tofu, mustard, turmeric, soy sauce, nutritional yeast, milk, salt, arrowroot, and oil to the blender and blend until smooth.

9. Transfer into the pan of greens and stir. Remove from heat.

10. Transfer into the spring form pan over the rice layer.

11. Bake at 375° F for about 35-40 minutes or until done. Remove from the oven and set aside.

Hummus Avocado Toast

Prep: 5 min	Total: 7 min	Servings: 2

Ingredients:

- 4 tablespoons hummus

- 4 slices vegan whole grain bread, toasted

- 1 avocado, peeled, pitted, sliced

- Pepper powder to taste

- Himalayan pink salt to taste

Instructions:

1. Apply a tablespoon of hummus on each of the bread slices.

2. Lay the avocado slices on it.

3. Season with Himalayan salt and pepper and serve immediately.

Ethiopian Tofu Scramble

Prep: 15 min	Total: 30 min	Servings: 6-8

Ingredients:

- 2 packages firm or extra firm tofu

- 2 large heads broccoli, chopped finely

- 4 cloves garlic, minced

- 1 avocado, peeled, pitted, chopped

- 2 injera, torn into pieces (optional)

- 1 teaspoons Berbere (Ethiopian spice blend) or to taste

- 1 teaspoon curry powder

- 1 teaspoon Hungarian paprika

- 1 teaspoon cumin

- 1/2 teaspoon dried thyme

- A large pinch cinnamon

- A large pinch ground cardamom

- A large pinch allspice

- A large pinch ground cloves

- 1 teaspoon salt, or to taste

- 1 tablespoon coconut oil

- 2 tablespoons fresh cilantro, chopped

Instructions:

1. Place a skillet over medium heat. Add coconut oil. When the oil is heated, add broccoli, and garlic and sauté for a couple of minutes.

2. Add tofu and sauté until brown. Stir frequently.

3. Mix berbere, 2-3 tablespoons of water, curry powder, cardamom, cinnamon, cloves, thyme, paprika, thyme, cumin, and allspice together in a bowl. Add it to the pan and mix well.

4. Add injera. Sauté for a couple of minutes until the mixture is almost dry.

5. Add avocado, mix well and serve.

Chapter 3: High Protein Vegan Salad Recipes

Black Bean Salad

Prep: 10 min	Total: 16 min	Servings: 6-8

Ingredients:

For salad:

- 2 cans (15 ounces each) black beans, drained, rinsed

- 2 cups fresh corn kernels

- 1/2 cup red onion, finely chopped

- 1 yellow bell pepper, chopped

- 1 orange bell pepper, chopped

- 1 large avocado, peeled, pitted, chopped

- 2 cups cherry tomatoes, chopped

- 1/2 cup fresh cilantro, chopped

- 2 tablespoons extra-virgin olive oil

- Salt to taste

- Pepper powder to taste

For the dressing:

- 6 tablespoons lime juice

- 2 cloves garlic, smashed

- 1/2 cup extra virgin olive oil

- Salt to taste

- 1/2 teaspoon chili powder

Instructions:

1. To make the dressing: Sprinkle a pinch of salt over the smashed garlic. Smash further until a coarse paste is formed.

2. Whisk together in a bowl, all the ingredients of the salad including the garlic paste and set aside.

3. Place a nonstick skillet over medium heat. Add oil. When the oil is heated, add corn, onions, and bell peppers and sauté until brown. Add black beans and heat until warm.

4. Add dressing and toss well. Season with salt and pepper.

5. Remove from heat. Add tomatoes, avocado, and cilantro and toss well.

6. Serve warm.

Lentil Salad

Prep: 15 min	Total: 17 min	Servings: 4

Ingredients:

- 2 cups cooked or canned lentils
- 2 cups cashew nuts, toasted
- 10-12 dried tomatoes
- 2 onions, chopped
- 2 jalapeños, chopped
- 3 cups arugula, chopped
- 6 tablespoons olive oil
- 6 slices vegan whole wheat bread, chopped into 1-inch cubes
- 1/4 cup raisins
- 4 tablespoons lemon juice or vinegar

- 2 tablespoons agave nectar (optional)

- Salt to taste

- Pepper powder to taste

Instructions:

1. Add all the ingredients except bread to a bowl and toss well.

2. Add bread just before serving. Toss well and serve.

Red Cabbage Salad

Prep: 15 min	Total: 25 min	Servings: 8

Ingredients:

For the salad:

- 2 packages (8 ounces each) seitan, chopped into strips of about 2 inches each
- 10-12 cups red cabbage, shredded
- 6 cloves garlic, minced
- 6 green onions, thinly sliced
- 2 small cucumbers, halved lengthwise, thinly sliced
- 2 tablespoons olive oil
- 2 teaspoons curry powder

For dressing:

- 2/3 cup creamy natural peanut butter
- 2/3 cup mango chutney
- 2/3 cup water

Instructions:

1. To make the dressing: Blend together all the ingredients for the dressing until smooth. Set aside until use.
2. Place a large skillet over medium heat. Add oil. When the oil is heated, add seitan and salt and sauté until brown.
3. Add garlic and sauté until fragrant. Add curry powder and sauté for a few seconds and remove from heat.
4. Mix together in a bowl cabbage and cucumber and toss.
5. Pour dressing on top and toss well.
6. Serve topped with seitan and green onions.

Carrot Slaw with Tempeh Triangles

Prep: 15 min	Total: 30 min	Servings: 8

Ingredients:

- 8 cups carrots, shredded

- 16 ounces tempeh, sliced into triangles

- 1 large onion, chopped

- 1/2 teaspoon liquid smoke (optional)

- 2 teaspoons extra virgin olive oil

- 6 tablespoons maple syrup, divided

- 4 teaspoons soy sauce

- 1/2 teaspoon turmeric powder

- 2 tablespoons curry powder

- Salt to taste

47

- Pepper powder to taste

- 4 - 5 tablespoons tahini

- 1/2 teaspoon cayenne pepper

- 1 cup flat leaf parsley, finely chopped + extra for garnishing

- 2 tablespoons walnuts, chopped

- 1/2 cup fresh lemon juice or apple cider vinegar

- 1/2 cup raisins (optional)

Instructions:

1. Place a skillet over high heat. Add oil. When the oil is heated, add tempeh, soy sauce, half the maple syrup, and liquid smoke.

2. Cook until the tempeh is brown and all the liquid in the skillet dries up. Remove from heat and set aside.

3. Mix together rest of the ingredients in a bowl and toss well. Serve topped with tempeh.

Edamame 'n Chickpea Salad

Prep: 15 min	Total: 20 min + chilling time	Servings: 3

Ingredients:

- 1/2 cup edamame

- 2 cups cooked or canned chickpeas, rinsed, drained

- 1 clove garlic, minced

- 1 small green bell pepper, chopped

- 1 small red bell pepper, chopped

- 1 medium carrot, chopped

- 2 tablespoons dried cranberries

For the dressing:

- 1 tablespoon olive oil

- 1 tablespoon grape seed oil

- 1/2 teaspoon sugar

- 1 teaspoon white vinegar

- 1/4 teaspoon dried basil

- 1/4 teaspoon dried oregano

- 1/4 teaspoon rosemary

- Salt to taste

- Pepper powder to taste

Instructions:

1. To make dressing: Add all the ingredients of the dressing to a bowl and whisk well.

2. Add rest of the ingredients to a bowl and toss well.

3. Pour dressing over the salad and toss well.

4. Chill and serve later.

Soy Bean and Fennel Salad

Prep: 10 min	Total: 12 min	Servings: 6

Ingredients:

- 6 cups cooked soy beans

- 16 cherry tomatoes, quartered

- 2 cups fennel bulb, sliced

- 1 large onion, minced

- 4 cloves garlic, peeled, pressed

- 1/3 cup fresh parsley, chopped

- 1/3 cup walnuts, chopped

- 1/3 cup fresh lemon juice

- 2 tablespoons extra virgin olive oil

- Salt to taste

- Pepper powder to taste

Instructions:

1. Add all the ingredients to a large bowl and toss well. Set aside for at least an hour before serving.

Chapter 4: High Protein Vegan Soup and Chili Recipes

Vegan Chili

Prep: 15 min	Total: 30 min	Servings: 4

Ingredients:

- 1 can (15 ounces) black beans, drained, rinsed

- ½ 15 ounces can kidney beans, drained, rinsed

- 1/2 tablespoon vegetable oil

- 1 jalapeño pepper, deseeded, minced

- 1 small onion, chopped

- 2 cloves garlic, minced

- 1/2 cup carrots, shredded

- 1/4 cup bulgur, rinsed

- 1 cup fresh tomatoes, chopped

- 1 tablespoon chili powder

- 3/4 cup tomato sauce

- 1/2 tablespoon ground cumin

- Salt to taste

- 2 tablespoons fresh cilantro, chopped

Instructions:

1. Place a heavy bottomed pot over medium heat. Add oil. When the oil is heated, add onions, carrots, and jalapeños and sauté until onions are translucent.
2. Add garlic and sauté until fragrant.
3. Add rest of the ingredients except cilantro and bring to the boil.
4. Lower heat, cover and simmer for about an hour.
5. Garnish with cilantro and serve.

Spicy Tofu and Vegetable Chili

Prep: 15 min	Total: 1 hr. 15 min	Servings: 6

Ingredients:

- ½ 15 ounces can cannellini or navy beans, drained, rinsed

- ½ 15 ounces can kidney beans, drained, rinsed

- 7 ounces extra firm tofu, crumbled

- 1 ½ tablespoon olive oil

- 1 medium onion, chopped

- ½ cup mushrooms, sliced

- 2 cloves garlic, minced

- ½ cup green bell pepper, chopped

- ½ cup zucchini, chopped

55

- 2 cups fresh tomatoes, chopped

- ½ cup celery, chopped

- 1 ½ tablespoons chili powder

- ¼ teaspoon cayenne pepper

- ¾ cup tomato sauce

- 1/2 tablespoon ground cumin

- 1 cup vegetable broth

- 1 ½ tablespoons sugar

- Salt to taste

- 2 tablespoons fresh cilantro, chopped

Instructions:

1. Place a heavy bottomed pot over medium heat. Add oil. When the oil is heated, add onions and garlic sauté until onions are golden brown.

2. Add rest of the ingredients except cilantro and bring to the boil.

3. Lower heat, cover and simmer for about an hour.

4. Garnish with cilantro and serve.

Lentil and Vegetable Soup

Prep: 15 min	Total: 55 min	Servings: 4

Ingredients:

- 1 medium onion, chopped
- 1 cup rutabaga, peeled, chopped
- 1 large carrot, peeled, chopped
- 1 ½ cups celeriac, peeled, chopped
- 4-5 ounces kale, discard hard stems and ribs, chopped
- 1/2 pound brown lentils, rinsed, soaked in water for a while
- 1 tablespoon olive oil
- 5 cups vegetable broth
- Salt to taste
- Pepper to taste

Instructions:

1. Place a heavy bottomed pot over medium heat. Add oil. When the oil is heated, add onions, carrots, celeriac, and rutabaga and sauté until onions are translucent.

2. Add rest of the ingredients and bring to the boil.

3. Lower heat, cover, and simmer until the lentils are tender.

4. Ladle into soup bowls and serve hot.

Spicy Black Bean Soup

Prep: 15 min	Total: 55 min	Servings: 6

Ingredients:

- 1 large onion, finely chopped

- 1- 2 jalapeño peppers, deseeded, minced

- 1 Hungarian pepper, deseeded, minced

- 3 carrots, peeled, chopped

- 3 cloves garlic, minced

- 3 cans (15 ounces each) black beans

- 1 1/2 teaspoons dried oregano

- 3 teaspoons freshly ground cumin

- 3 tablespoons olive oil

- 6 cups vegetable stock

- Salt to taste

- Pepper powder to taste

- 2 tablespoons fresh cilantro, chopped

Instructions:

1. Mash about 1 1/2 cans of black beans. Add garlic to it and stir. Set aside.

2. Place a heavy bottomed pot over medium heat. Add oil. When the oil is heated, add onions, carrots, peppers, cumin, and oregano and sauté until the vegetables are soft.

3. Add rest of the ingredients except cilantro and bring to the boil.

4. Ladle into soup bowls and serve hot, garnished with cilantro.

Miso Soup

Prep: 5 min	Total: 15 min	Servings: 6

Ingredients

- 2 cups firm tofu, chopped
- 4 tablespoons miso paste
- 6 cups vegetable broth
- 1 cup green onions, chopped
- 1 cup chard, chopped
- Salt to taste
- Pepper powder to taste

Instructions

1. Add miso paste to a bowl. Add about 1/2 cup of warm broth and whisk well.

2. Place a large saucepan or pot over medium heat.

3. Add stock and bring to a boil.

4. Add rest of the ingredients and stir.

5. Simmer for 5-7 minutes.

6. Ladle into soup bowls and serve warm.

Split Pea Soup

Prep: 15 min	Total: 55 min	Servings: 6

Ingredients:

- 1 1/2 cups green split peas, rinsed, soaked in water overnight
- 1 medium white onion, chopped
- 1 large carrot, sliced
- 3 stalks celery, sliced
- 1 1/2 teaspoons ground cumin
- Sea Kelp delight seasoning to taste
- 4 tablespoons liquid aminos or soy sauce to taste
- 14-15 cups water

Instructions

1. Place all the ingredients in a large pot and stir. Place the pot over medium heat.

63

2. Cook until the split peas are tender. Add more water if required.

3. Mix well. Ladle into soup bowls and serve hot.

Hearty Winter Vegetable Soup

Prep: 15 min	Total: 55 min	Servings: 6

Ingredients:

- 1 cup red lentils, rinsed, soaked overnight

- 1/2 cup lima beans, rinsed, soaked overnight

- 1 onion, diced

- 8 cherry tomatoes, whole

- 1 medium carrot, peeled, sliced

- 2 stalks celery, sliced

- 1 small Serrano chili pepper, chopped

- 2 cloves garlic, minced

- 1/4 teaspoon paprika or to taste

- Sea salt to taste

- Pepper powder to taste

- 1/2 teaspoon curry powder or to taste

- 3 tablespoons liquid aminos or to taste

- 2 tablespoons parsley, chopped

- 4 cups water

Instructions:

1. Place all the ingredients in a large pot and stir. Place the pot over medium heat.

2. Cook until the lentils and lima beans are tender. Add more water if required.

3. Mix well. Ladle into bowls and serve hot.

Chapter 5: High Protein Vegan Appetizer Recipes

Mushroom Tapenade

Prep: 15 min	Total: 30 min	Servings: 6-8

Ingredients:

- 4 cups shiitake mushrooms, quartered

- 6 cups cremini mushrooms, quartered

- 2/3 cup oil-cured black olives, pitted

- 6 cloves garlic, minced

- 2 tablespoons fresh parsley, chopped

- 2 tablespoons fresh thyme chopped

- 2 tablespoons capers, drained, rinsed

- 4 tablespoons extra virgin olive oil

- 1/2 teaspoon salt

- 1/2 teaspoon pepper powder

- 1/2 cup dry white wine

Instructions:

1. Place a large skillet over medium-high heat. Add half the oil. When the oil is heated, add garlic, thyme, salt, and pepper and sauté until light brown. Stir frequently.

2. Add mushrooms and sauté until soft. Add wine and cook until dry.

3. Remove from heat and cool for a while.

4. Add mushroom mixture, olives, capers, parsley, and remaining oil into a food processor. Pulse until well-combined rough mixture is formed.

5. Serve at room temperature.

Caprese on a Stick

Prep: 10 min	Total: 20 min	Servings: 8-10

Ingredients:

- 2 pints cherry tomatoes, halved
- 2 packages (16 ounces each) firm tofu, chopped into bite-sized cubes
- 12 ounces fresh basil leaves
- 6 tablespoons olive oil
- Salt to taste
- Pepper powder to taste

For balsamic glaze:

- 1 1/2 cups balsamic vinegar
- 4 tablespoons brown sugar (optional)

Instructions:

69

1. Add brown sugar and vinegar to a saucepan. Place the saucepan over high heat. Boil until the solution reduces to a syrup-like consistency. Remove from heat.

2. Take a few toothpicks or cocktail sticks. Thread the tomatoes, basil, and tofu onto it in any manner you desire. If the basil leaf is large, fold and then thread it.

3. Drizzle oil over it.

4. Serve with balsamic glaze either as a dip or drizzle it over the sticks.

Breaded, Spiced Tofu

Prep: 15 min	Total: 30 min	Servings: 6-8

Ingredients:

- 2 packages (16 ounces each) extra firm tofu, drained, pressed of excess moisture

- 1 cup all-purpose flour

- 4 cups vegetable broth

- 6 tablespoons nutritional yeast

- 6 tablespoons vegetable oil or more if required

- 2 teaspoons sage

- 1 teaspoon freshly ground black pepper

- 1 1/2 teaspoons salt or to taste

- 1 teaspoon cayenne pepper

Instructions:

1. Chop the tofu into 1/2-inch thick and 1/2-inch-wide strips.

2. Add tofu to a large bowl and pour broth over it. Set it aside for about 30 minutes.

3. Mix together in a bowl, flour, nutritional yeast, salt, pepper, sage, and cayenne pepper.

4. Add oil to a skillet and place over medium-high heat.

5. Remove the tofu strips from the broth and press out most of the liquid from it.

6. Dredge the strips in the flour mixture. Coat it well.

7. When the oil is heated, add a few tofu strips and cook until golden brown. Remove with a slotted spoon and place on paper towels.

8. Cook in batches. Add more oil if required. Serve with a dip of your choice.

Mini Bean Burgers

Prep: 10 min	Total: 40 min	Servings: 4-6

Ingredients:

- 3/4 cup water

- 1/2 cup uncooked quick oats

- 1 tablespoon olive oil + more for frying

- 1 onion, finely chopped

- 1 carrot, finely chopped

- 2 cloves garlic, minced

- 1 tablespoon water

- 1/2 stalk celery, chopped

- 1/2 teaspoon dried basil

- 1/2 teaspoon salt

- 1 cup cooked adzuki beans

- 2 tablespoons fresh parsley, chopped

- 6 tablespoons brown rice flour

Instructions:

1. Add 3/4-cup water to a saucepan and bring to the boil. Add oats and simmer until thickened.

2. Place a skillet over medium heat. Add olive oil. When the oil is heated, add carrots, onions, celery, and garlic. Sauté until the vegetables are tender.

3. Add a tablespoon of water, basil and salt. Cover and cook until dry.

4. Let it cool a bit. Transfer the entire contents into the blender. Add adzuki beans and blend until smooth. Add parsley and pulse for a few seconds. Transfer into a bowl.

5. Add rice flour mixture and mix well. Divide into small balls and shape into patties.

6. Place a nonstick skillet. Add about 2 tablespoons olive oil. Add the patties and fry on both the sides until golden brown. Serve hot with a dip of your choice.

Salted Crispy Almonds

Prep: 8 hrs.	Total: 10 hrs.	Servings: 15-20

Ingredients:

- 2 pounds raw almonds
- 2 tablespoons sea salt
- 1 teaspoon chili powder
- Filtered water as required

Instructions:

1. Place the almonds in a bowl. Add water such that the almonds are totally soaked in it. It should cover at least 2 inches above the almonds.

2. Add salt and mix well. Leave overnight.

3. Drain the water and sprinkle more salt over the almonds. Sprinkle chili powder.

76

4. Bake in a preheated oven at 170° F for a couple of hours or until light brown and crisp.

5. Turn the almonds around a couple of times while baking.

6. Store it in an airtight container.

Pecan Pie Balls

Prep: 10 min	Total: 20 min	Servings: 12-15

Ingredients:

- 2 cups dates, pitted
- 2 cups pecans
- 1 teaspoon sea salt
- 1 teaspoon pure vanilla extract

Instructions:

1. Place all the ingredients in a food processor. Pulse until it forms a dough.
2. Remove from the food processor and place in a bowl.
3. Divide the mixture and form into small balls. Refrigerate and serve.

Falafel

Prep: 10 min	Total: 30 min	Servings: 4

Ingredients:

- ½ 15.5 ounce can of chickpeas, rinsed, drained

- 2 cups collard greens (stemmed and torn)

- 2 cloves garlic, chopped

- 1 tablespoon tahini paste

- 1 tablespoon fresh lemon juice

- 1/2 teaspoon cumin

- Sea salt to taste

- Black pepper powder to taste

- 2 tablespoons oat flour

- 2 tablespoons olive oil for cooking or more if required

Instructions

1. Place greens, chickpeas, garlic, tahini, lemon juice, and cumin in the food processor. Pulse until it forms a dough-like consistency. Transfer into a bowl.

2. Add oat flour and mix well. Divide the dough into small balls of about 1 1/2-inch diameter and shape into small patties.

3. Place a nonstick pan over medium heat. Add oil. Place 3-4 falafels on the pan and cook until golden brown on both the sides. Cook in batches. Add more oil if required.

4. Serve hot with hummus.

Chapter 6: High Protein Vegan Main Course

Vegan Taco

Prep: 10 min	Total: 30 min	Servings: 3

Ingredients:

- ½ 12-ounce package soy chorizo, discard casing

- 1 onion, sliced

- 1 onion, chopped

- ½ 15.5-ounce can vegan refried black beans, heated

- 1 jalapeño, deseeded, minced

- 6 corn tortillas, warmed according to the instructions on the package

- 1 teaspoon olive oil

- 2 tablespoons fresh cilantro, chopped

- Salt to taste

Instructions:

1. Place a skillet over medium heat. Add oil. When the oil is heated, add sliced onions and jalapeño and sauté until the onions are translucent.

2. Add soy chorizo and cook until brown, breaking it simultaneously.

3. Place 3 tortillas on your work area. Spread about 2 tablespoons of refried beans over it.

4. Place the remaining tortillas over it. Spread some more of the refried beans over it.

5. Divide and place the soy chorizo mixture over the second tortilla. Sprinkle chopped onions and cilantro over it.

6. Serve immediately.

Sun-Dried Tomato, Mushroom, Spinach, and Tofu Quiche

Prep: 30 min	Total: 1 hrs. 20 min	Servings: 4

Ingredients:

For the crust:

- 1/2 cup rolled oats or buckwheat groats, ground into flour

- 1/2 cup almonds, ground into flour

- 1/2 teaspoon dried oregano

- 1/2 teaspoon dried parsley

- 2 teaspoons ground flax mixed with 2 tablespoons water

- 2 teaspoons coconut oil or olive oil

- 1/4 teaspoon salt

- 1 tablespoon water or more if required

For the quiche:

- 2 teaspoons coconut oil or olive oil

- 1 1/2 cups cremini mushrooms, sliced

- 7 ounces firm tofu, pressed of excess moisture

- 1 tablespoon almond milk or more if required

- 1 leek, thinly sliced

- 1/4 cup fresh basil, minced

- 1/4 cup fresh chives, minced

- 1/2 cup baby spinach

- 1/4 cup oil-packed, sun-dried tomatoes, finely chopped

- 2 cloves garlic, minced

- 1/2 teaspoon dried oregano

- 1/2 teaspoon red chili flakes or to taste

- 1 tablespoon nutritional yeast

- Salt to taste

- Pepper powder to taste

Instructions:

1. To make the crust: Mix together the ground flaxseeds and water and set aside for a while.

2. Mix together in a bowl, almond meal, oat flour, parsley, oregano, and salt. Add water, flaxseed mixture, and oil.

3. Mix until well combined to form a sticky dough.

4. Grease a pie dish and transfer the dough into it. Spread it on the bottom of the dish and sides and press well.

5. Prick with a fork at different places in the crust.

6. Bake in a preheated oven at 350° F for about 15 minutes or until light brown and firm.

7. To make the filling: Crumble the tofu into a blender. Add almond milk and blend until smooth and creamy. Add more milk if required.

8. Place a skillet over medium-high heat. Add oil. When the oil is heated, add leek and garlic and sauté until translucent.

9. Add mushrooms, and salt and cook until most of the moisture dries up.

10. Add rest of the ingredients except tofu. Cook until the spinach wilts.

11. Remove from heat and add tofu and mix well. Taste and adjust the seasoning if necessary.

12. Transfer this mixture over the crust. Spread it all over the crust evenly.

13. Bake in a preheated oven at 350° F for about 15 minutes or until light brown and firm.

14. Remove from oven and cool for a while.

15. Cut into wedges and serve warm.

Quinoa Falafel with Avocado-Tahini Dressing

Prep: 15 min	Total: 30 min	Servings: 6-8

Ingredients:

For falafel:

- 1 cup cooked quinoa

- 3 cups cooked chickpeas, rinsed, drained

- 1 large onion, finely chopped

- 2 tablespoons ground cumin

- 2 tablespoons flaxseed meal mixed with 4 tablespoons water

- 1/2 teaspoon salt or to taste

- Pepper powder to taste

- 1/4 cup vegetable oil or more if required

For avocado tahini dressing:

- 1/2 cup tahini

- 2 ripe avocados, peeled, pitted, chopped

- 1/4 cup fresh cilantro

- 3 tablespoons lime juice

- 1 cup water

Instructions:

1. To make dressing: Add all the ingredients of the dressing to a blender and blend until smooth. Transfer to a bowl and set aside.

2. To make falafel: Mix together flaxseed meal and water in a small bowl and set it aside for a while.

3. Add chickpeas to a food processor and pulse until well mashed. Transfer into a large bowl.

4. Place a skillet over medium heat. Add about 2 tablespoons oil. Add onions and garlic and sauté until onions are translucent.

5. Remove from heat. Transfer to the bowl of chickpeas. Add rest of the ingredients along with flaxseed mixture. Mix well.

6. Divide the mixture into 24 balls and shape into patties.

7. Fry the falafel in batches.

8. Place a nonstick skillet over medium heat. Add about 1-2 tablespoons oil. When the oil is heated, place 3-4 falafels over it and cook until the underside is brown. Flip sides and cook the other side, too.

9. Remove onto a plate and serve with avocado tahini dressing and pita bread and a few slices of tomatoes.

Veggie & Tofu Noodle Bowl

Prep: 15 min	Total: 40 min	Servings: 6

Ingredients:

- 1 large head broccoli

- 1 1/3 pounds firm tofu

- 2 large onions, thinly sliced

- 1 red bell pepper, deseeded, thinly sliced

- 1 yellow bell pepper, deseeded, thinly sliced

- 1 orange bell pepper, deseeded, thinly sliced

- 9 ounces whole wheat spaghetti

- 2 cups mushrooms, sliced

- 3 cloves garlic, minced

- 4 tablespoons dark brown sugar

- 3 tablespoons soy sauce

- 3 tablespoons rice vinegar

- 1 1/2 tablespoons sesame oil, toasted

- 1/2 cup creamy peanut butter

- 1 teaspoon red chili flakes

- 2 tablespoons sesame seeds

- 2 tablespoons vegetable oil

- Salt to taste

Instructions:

1. Chop the broccoli into florets. Peel the stem and slice the stem.

2. Place a large pot of water over medium-high heat. Add 1 ½-teaspoons salt and bring to the boil.

3. Add pasta and cook for a couple of minutes. Add broccoli and stems and cook until al dente. Drain and set aside. Retain about a cup of the cooking water.

4. Whisk together in a bowl peanut butter, brown sugar, rice vinegar, soy sauce, sesame oil, garlic, and red pepper flakes and set aside.

5. Rinse the spaghetti under cold running water. Drain and set aside.

6. Place a wok over medium-high heat. Add 1-tablespoon vegetable oil. When oil is heated, add tofu and sauté until light brown. Remove the tofu onto a plate and set aside.

7. Add remaining vegetable oil to the wok. When the oil is heated, add onions and garlic and sauté for a couple of minutes. Add bell peppers and mushrooms. Sauté until soft.

8. Add tofu, spaghetti, and broccoli and stir-fry for a couple of minutes. Add peanut butter mixture and the retained water. Mix well and heat thoroughly.

9. Serve in individual bowls topped with sesame seeds.

Spinach with Pasta

Prep: 15 min	Total: 30 min	Servings: 6

Ingredients:

- 2 cups portabella mushroom caps, sliced

- 8 ounces of vegan sausages, discard casing, chopped

- 1 cup onions, chopped

- 1/2 cup red wine

- 2 tablespoons olive oil

- 2 cloves garlic, minced

- Salt to taste

- Black pepper powder to taste

- 1 teaspoon oregano

- 2 ounces of whole wheat penne pasta, cook according to the instructions on the package
- 4 cups spinach leaves
- 2 tablespoons balsamic vinegar
- 2 tablespoons vegan cheddar cheese

Instructions:

1. Place a large skillet over medium heat. Add oil. When the oil is heated, add onions and garlic. Sauté for a couple of minutes. Add mushrooms and sauté for a while until the vegetables are slightly brown.
2. Add red wine. Mix well.
3. Add sausages, salt, pepper, and oregano. Add pasta and toss.
4. To serve: Place the spinach on a serving platter. Place the pasta along with the sausages over the spinach. Sprinkle balsamic vinegar and cheese and serve.

Kale Broccoli Chickpea Orecchiette Pasta

Prep: 10 min	Total: 30 min	Servings: 6

Ingredients:

- 12 ounces Orecchiette pasta

- 1 1/2 cans (15 ounces each) chickpeas, rinsed, drained

- 3 tablespoons olive oil

- 5 cloves garlic, finely chopped

- 5 cups kale, discard stems and ribs, chopped

- 3/4 cup cherry tomatoes, sliced

- 1 1/2 cups broccoli florets, chopped

- 1 shallot, chopped

- 3 3/4 cups vegetable broth

- 1 1/2 teaspoons dried basil

- 1 1/2 teaspoons dried oregano

- 1/2 cup nondairy milk of your choice

96

- 1 teaspoon red chili flakes or to taste + extra to garnish

- 3/4 cup vegan parmesan cheese + extra for garnish

- Salt to taste

- Pepper powder to taste

- 2 tablespoons fresh parsley, chopped

Instructions:

1. Place a large skillet over medium-high heat. Add oil. When the oil is heated, add shallot and garlic and sauté until fragrant.

2. Add Orecchiette pasta, stock, milk, basil, oregano, chili flakes, and broccoli and bring to the boil.

3. Lower heat, cover and simmer for about 9 minutes.

4. Add tomatoes and chickpeas and mix. Cook for 6 minutes.

5. Add kale and simmer uncovered until kale wilts and the liquid almost dry.

6. Add cheese and stir. Remove from heat.

7. Serve garnished with cheese, parsley, and red pepper flakes. Serve with toasted vegan bread.

Tofu Club Sandwich

Prep: 15 min	Total: 40 min	Servings: 6

Ingredients:

- 2 packages tofu, chopped into 5 mm slices

- 12 slices vegan bread, toasted

- A few lettuce leaves

- 1 avocado, peeled, pitted, sliced

- 1 cup onions, sliced

- 4 cloves garlic, minced

- 1 tablespoon oil

- 2 sprigs of fresh rosemary or 2 teaspoons dried rosemary

- A few fresh basil leaves

- 2 tomatoes, sliced

- A little mustard sauce

- 1/2 cup tahini to spread

- Salt to taste

Instructions:

1. Place a pan over medium heat. Add oil. When the oil is hot, add onions and garlic. Sauté until the onions are translucent.

2. Add tofu. Fry until golden brown. Flip sides and cook the other side until golden brown. Remove from heat and keep aside.

3. Spread tahini on one side of all the slices of bread.

4. Lay lettuce leaves on 6 slices of bread. Place a little mustard over the lettuce. Lay the tomato slices, avocado, and tofu.

5. Lay 3-4 basil leaves and cover with remaining 6 bread slices. Slice into the shape you desire and serve.

Lentil & Bulgur Pilaf

Prep: 15 min	Total: 1 hr. 10 min	Servings: 8

Ingredients:

- 9 cups low sodium vegetable broth

- 2 1/2 cups brown lentils, rinsed

- 1 large onion, chopped

- 2 bay leaves

- 1/2 teaspoon salt, or to taste

- 1 teaspoon allspice powder

- Freshly ground pepper, to taste

- 1 1/2 cups coarse bulgur

- 1/4 cup lemon juice

- 2 tablespoons extra-virgin olive oil

- 2 small yellow squash, halved lengthwise and cut into slices

- 2 small zucchinis, halved lengthwise, cut into slices

- 2 cups mushrooms, sliced

- 4 cloves garlic, minced

- 4 teaspoons freshly grated lemon zest

- 1/4 cup fresh parsley, chopped

- 1//4 cup chopped fresh cilantro or dill

Instructions:

1. Place a large saucepan over medium heat. Add lentils, onions, bay leaves, salt, allspice, pepper, and broth. Bring to a boil.

2. Lower heat. Cover the saucepan and simmer for 20 minutes.

3. Add bulgur. Cook until the lentils and bulgur are cooked and the broth is dried up.

4. Remove the bay leaves and discard it.

5. To the pilaf, add lemon juice and mix well.

6. Meanwhile, place a nonstick skillet over medium heat. Add oil. When oil is heated, add zucchini, squash, mushrooms, garlic,

and lemon zest. Sauté for 4-5 minutes or until the vegetables are tender.

7. Add parsley, cilantro, salt, and pepper. Mix well.

8. Place the pilaf on individual serving plates. Place the vegetables over it and serve.

Peanut Tofu Wrap

Prep: 10 min	Total: 15 min	Servings: 4

Ingredients:

- 4 tablespoons Thai peanut sauce

- 4 (8 inches each) whole wheat flour tortillas

- 1 cup red bell pepper, sliced

- 8 snow peas, thinly sliced

- 8 ounces baked, seasoned tofu, thinly sliced

Instructions:

1. Place the tortillas on your work area. Spread about 1 tablespoon of peanut sauce on each of the tortillas.

2. Place tofu, bell pepper slices, and snow peas slices in the center. Roll and serve.

Shepherd's Pie

Prep: 15 min	Total: 60 min	Servings: 6

Ingredients:

For mashed potatoes layer:

- 1 1/2 pounds Yukon gold potatoes, thoroughly washed, halved
- 2 tablespoons vegan butter
- Salt to taste
- Pepper powder to taste

For the lentil layer:

- 3/4 cup green lentils, rinsed, drained
- 2 cups vegetable stock
- 1 onion, chopped

- 1 clove garlic, minced

- 5-ounce bag mixed frozen vegetables

- 1/2 teaspoon dried thyme

- 1/2 tablespoon olive oil

Instructions:

1. Place a large pot of water over medium heat. Add potatoes and salt and cook until done. Drain well and transfer into a bowl.

2. Mash with a potato masher until smooth. Add vegan butter, salt, and pepper. Partially cover and keep aside.

3. Place a large saucepan over medium heat. Add oil. When the oil is heated, add onions and garlic and sauté until light golden brown

4. Add green lentils, vegetable stock, frozen vegetables, and thyme and bring to the boil.

5. Lower heat, cover, and cook until lentils are almost cooked. Add vegetables, mix well, cover and cook for 10-15 minutes. Uncover and dry up the remaining moisture.

6. Transfer the lentils to a greased baking dish. Layer with the mashed potato layer.

7. Bake in a preheated oven at 425° F for about 15 minutes or until light brown on top.

8. Serve hot.

Black Beans & Rice

Prep: 5 min	Total: 30 min	Servings: 4

Ingredients:

- 1 teaspoon olive oil

- 1 onion, chopped

- 1 clove garlic, minced

- 1/2 cup uncooked white rice

- 1 cup low-sodium and low-fat vegetable stock

- Cayenne pepper to taste

- 1/2 teaspoon ground cumin

- 1 3/4 cups canned black beans, drained

Instructions:

1. Place a stockpot over medium heat. Add oil. When oil is heated add onion and garlic and sauté. When the onions are lightly browned add rice and sauté for a couple of minutes.

2. Add vegetable broth. When it starts boiling, cover and lower heat and cook until the rice is done.

3. Add spices and black beans. Serve hot.

Chapter 7: High Protein Vegan Side Dish Recipes

Broccoli & Black Beans Stir Fry

Prep: 10 min	Total: 20 min	Servings: 6

Ingredients:

- 4 cups broccoli florets

- 2 cups cooked black beans

- 1 tablespoon sesame oil

- 4 teaspoons sesame seeds

- 2 cloves garlic, finely minced

- 2 teaspoons ginger, finely chopped

- A large pinch red chili flakes

- A pinch turmeric powder

- Salt to taste

- Lime juice to taste (optional)

Instructions:

1. Steam broccoli for 6 minutes. Drain and set aside.

2. Warm the sesame oil in a large frying pan over medium heat. Add sesame seeds, chili flakes, ginger, garlic, turmeric powder, and salt. Sauté for a couple of minutes.

3. Add broccoli and black beans and sauté until thoroughly heated.

4. Sprinkle lime juice and serve hot.

Stuffed Peppers

Prep: 10 min	Total: 35 min	Servings: 8

Ingredients:

- 2 cans (15 ounces each) black beans, drained, rinsed

- 2 cups tofu, pressed, crumbled

- 3/4 cup green onions, thinly sliced

- 1/2 cup fresh cilantro, chopped

- 1/4 cup vegetable oil

- 1/4 cup lime juice

- 3 cloves garlic, finely chopped

- 1/2 teaspoon salt

- 1/2 teaspoon chili powder

- 8 large bell peppers, halved lengthwise, deseeded

- 3 Roma tomatoes, diced

Instructions:

1. Mix together in a bowl all the ingredients except the bell peppers to make the filling.

2. Fill the peppers with this mixture.

3. Cut 8 aluminum foils of size 18 x 12 inches. Place 2 halves on each aluminum foil. Seal the peppers such that there is a gap on the sides.

4. Grill under direct heat for about 15 minutes.

5. Sprinkle with some cilantro and serve.

Sweet 'n Spicy Tofu

Prep: 15 min	Total: 35 min	Servings: 8

Ingredients:

- 14 ounces extra firm tofu; press the excess liquid and chop into cubes.

- 3 tablespoons olive oil

- 2 2-3 cloves garlic, minced

- 4 tablespoons Sriracha sauce or any other hot sauce

- 2 tablespoons soy sauce

- 1/4 cup sweet chili sauce

- 5-6 cups mixed vegetables of your choice (like carrots, cauliflower, broccoli, potato, etc.)

- Salt to taste (optional)

Instructions:

1. Place a nonstick pan over medium-high heat. Add 1 tablespoon oil. When oil is hot, add garlic and mixed vegetables and stir-fry until crisp and tender. Remove and keep aside.

2. Place the pan back on heat. Add 2 tablespoons oil. When oil is hot, add tofu and sauté until golden brown. Add the sautéed vegetables. Mix well and remove from heat.

3. Make a mixture of sauces by mixing together all the sauces in a small bowl.

4. Serve the stir fried vegetables and tofu with sauce.

Eggplant & Mushrooms in Peanut Sauce

Prep: 15 min	Total: 32 min	Servings: 6

Ingredients:

- 4 Japanese eggplants cut into 1-inch thick round slices

- 3/4 pounds of shiitake mushrooms, stems discarded, halved

- 3 tablespoons smooth peanut butter

- 2 1/2 tablespoons rice vinegar

- 1 1/2 tablespoons soy sauce

- 1 1/2 tablespoons, peeled, fresh ginger, finely grated

- 1 1/2 tablespoons light brown sugar

- Coarse salt to taste

- 3 scallions, cut into 2-inch lengths, thinly sliced lengthwise

Instructions:

1. Place the eggplants and mushroom in a steamer. Steam the eggplant and mushrooms until tender. Transfer to a bowl.

2. To a small bowl, add peanut butter and vinegar and whisk.

3. Add rest of the ingredients and whisk well. Add this to the bowl of eggplant slices. Add scallions and mix well.

4. Serve hot.

Green Beans Stir Fry

Prep: 15 min	Total: 30 min	Servings: 6-8

Ingredients:

- 1 1/2 pounds of green beans, stringed, chopped into 1 ½-inch pieces

- 1 large onion, thinly sliced

- 4 star anise (optional)

- 3 tablespoons avocado oil

- 1 1/2 tablespoons tamari sauce or soy sauce

- Salt to taste

- 3/4 cup water

Instructions:

1. Place a wok over medium heat. Add oil. When oil is heated, add onions and sauté until onions are translucent.

117

2. Add beans, water, tamari sauce, and star anise and stir. Cover and cook until the beans are tender.

3. Uncover, add salt and raise the heat to high. Cook until the water dries up in the wok. Stir a couple of times while cooking.

Collard Greens 'n Tofu

Prep: 15 min	Total: 40 min	Servings: 4

Ingredients:

- 2 pounds of collard greens, rinsed, chopped

- 1 cup water

- 1/2 pound of tofu, chopped

- Salt to taste

- Pepper powder to taste

- Crushed red chili to taste

Instructions:

1. Place a large skillet over medium-high heat. Add oil. When the oil is heated, add tofu and cook until brown.

2. Add rest of the ingredients and mix well.

3. Cook until greens wilts and almost dry.

119

Chapter 8: High Protein Vegan Dessert Recipes

Red Velvet Protein Bites

Prep: 10 min	Total: 15 min + chilling time	Servings: 10

Ingredients:

- 1/2 cup almond meal or almond flour

- 6 tablespoons coconut flour

- 2 teaspoons beetroot powder

- 6 tablespoons plant-based vanilla protein powder

- 4 tablespoons cocoa powder

- 3/4 cup dairy-free dark chocolate

- 6 tablespoons almond milk

- 2 teaspoons vanilla extract

- 2 tablespoons coconut oil, melted

Instructions:

1. Mix together in a bowl, almond meal, coconut flour, beetroot powder, and protein powder.

2. Add rest of the ingredients and mix well.

3. Transfer onto a lined baking sheet and spread well with a rolling pin.

4. Freeze for 15 minutes.

5. Meanwhile, melt dark chocolate in a microwave.

6. Remove the baking sheet from the freezer and chop into squares. Dip the squares into the melted chocolate and place it back on the baking sheet.

7. Chill again and serve.

Coconut Chia Pudding

Prep: 5 min	Total: 7 min + chilling time	Servings: 4

Ingredients:

- 4 cups coconut milk, unsweetened
- 3 tablespoons agave nectar
- 1 cup chia seeds
- 1 large mango, peeled, pitted, chopped

Instructions:

1. Add milk, agave nectar, and chia seeds to a bowl and stir. Transfer into individual dessert bowls.

2. Chill for 5-6 hours.

3. Top with mango and serve.

Plum Protein Parfait

Prep: 20 min	Total: 60 min + chilling time	Servings: 6

Ingredients:

For the plum layer:

- 4 cups plums, pitted, chopped

- 2 tablespoons maple syrup

- 1 teaspoon vanilla extract

For the coconut cream layer:

- 1/2 cup coconut milk

- 2 small bananas, sliced, frozen

For the chia pudding layer:

- 8 tablespoons chia seeds

- 2 tablespoons ground cinnamon

- 2 cups soy milk or almond milk

- 4 tablespoons maple syrup

- 2 teaspoons ground ginger

For the crumble layer:

- 1 cup whole wheat flour

- 2 cups oats

- 1/2 cup almond milk or soy milk

- 8 Medjool dates, pitted

- 4 tablespoons coconut oil, melted

- 6 tablespoons shredded coconut, unsweetened

Instructions:

1. To make crumble layer: Mix oats and flour together in a bowl.

2. Blend together the rest of the ingredients of the crumble layer until smooth. Add this mixture into the bowl of oats and stir.

125

3. Transfer the ingredients to a greased baking dish.

4. Bake in a preheated oven at 400° F for about 15 minutes or until golden brown on top.

5. Remove from the oven. When cool enough to handle, crumble it and bake until crunchy.

6. To make plum layer: Mix together plum, maple syrup, and vanilla and set aside.

7. To make chia pudding layer: Add all the ingredients of this layer to a bowl and stir and set aside.

8. To make coconut cream layer: Add coconut milk and banana slices to a blender and blend until smooth.

9. To assemble: Take 6 glasses or masons jars. Divide and spoon in the plum mixture to make the bottom layer.

10. Next layer with coconut cream layer, followed by the chia pudding layer, and finally top with the crumble layer.

11. Chill and serve.

Dragon Fruit Pudding

Prep: 10 min	Total: 25 min + chilling time	Servings: 4

Ingredients:

For the pudding:

- 7 ounces of frozen dragon fruit puree

- 2 cups frozen chopped mango

- 1 kiwi, peeled, chopped

- 2 cups frozen pineapple

- 2 cups baby spinach

- 1 cup almond milk or soy milk, unsweetened

- 4 tablespoons agave nectar

- 4 scoops vanilla pea protein powder

For the topping:

- 1/2 cup blackberries

- 1/2 cup blueberries

- 1 banana, sliced

- 4 tablespoons pumpkin seeds

- 4 tablespoons almonds, chopped

- 4 teaspoons chia seeds

Instructions:

1. Add all the ingredients of the pudding to a blender and blend until smooth.

2. Transfer into dessert bowls. Chill for an hour.

3. Meanwhile toast the almonds and pumpkin seeds.

4. Remove from the refrigerator. Top with blackberries, blueberries, banana, almonds, pumpkin seeds, and chia seeds.

5. Serve immediately.

Puffed Quinoa Peanut Butter Balls

Prep: 5 min	Total: 15 min + chilling time	Servings: 8

Ingredients:

- 2 cups puffed quinoa
- 1 cup peanut butter
- 1/2 cup agave nectar
- 2 tablespoons crushed peanuts
- 2 teaspoons vanilla extract
- Dairy-free dark chocolate, melted (optional)

Instructions:

1. Mix together in a heatproof bowl, peanut butter, agave, and vanilla. Place the bowl in a double boiler for a while until the ingredients are softened and smooth flowing.

129

2. Remove from heat and add puffed quinoa. Mix well and refrigerate for 15-20 minutes.

3. Remove from the refrigerator and form small balls. Dip into dark chocolate if desired. Refrigerate again for 15 minutes before serving.

Chocó-Berry Cheese Cake

Prep: 10 min	Total: 25 min + chilling time	Servings: 8

Ingredients:

For the crust:

- 1 1/2 cups porridge oats

- 6 tablespoons almond milk

- 1/2 teaspoon cocoa powder

- A large pinch salt

For the cream layer:

- 4 cups cannellini beans

- ½ cup almond milk

- 4 teaspoons stevia or any sweetener of your choice

- 2 scoops pea protein powder

- 1 teaspoon vanilla extract

For the chocolate layer:

- 1 tablespoon cocoa powder

- 2 teaspoons stevia

- 2 tablespoons almond milk

For the berry layer:

- 1 cup berries

- 2 teaspoons stevia

- 1 scoop pea protein powder

Instructions:

1. To make the crust: Mix together all of the ingredients for the crust. Transfer into a cake tin. Press well.

2. To make the cream layer: Add the cannellini beans, almond milk, stevia, pea protein powder, and vanilla to a food processor. Pulse until well combined. Remove from the food processor and

take out about a cup of the mixture and keep in a bowl. To this, add the chocolate layer ingredients.

3. Spread this chocolate layer over the prepared crust.

4. To the remaining beans mixture, add berries and sweetener to it. Blend until smooth.

5. Spread over the chocolate layer.

6. Garnish with berries and sprinkle the coconut flakes.

7. Refrigerate until well chilled. Chop into wedges and serve.

Easy Chocó-Nut Ice cream

Prep: 5 min	Total: 15 min + freezing time	Servings: 8

Ingredients:

- 6 bananas, sliced, frozen
- 1/2 cup creamy peanut butter
- 1/2 cup unsweetened cocoa powder
- 3 teaspoons vanilla extract
- Agave nectar or sweetener of your choice to taste

Instructions:

1. Blend together all the ingredients in a blender until smooth. Transfer into a bowl. Using a hand mixer, beat it until fluffy.

2. Pour the mixture into a freezer-safe container and freeze until done.

134

Conclusion

I thank you once again for choosing this book and hope you had a good time reading it and experimenting in your kitchen. The main aim of this book was to educate you on the basics of the vegan diet and provide you with delicious high protein vegan recipes.

As you can see, it is quite easy for you to prepare these recipes and share the process with family members and friends. The protein-rich vegan diet is easily the healthiest vegetarian diet in the world and is sure to help you attain all your health goals. But it is important for you to keep up with the diet consistently. You must turn it into a lifestyle choice and pursue it until you get the results you want.

If you are finding it hard to make the transition, then you can ask a partner to join in, as that can motivate you to keep up with the diet for a long time. Once you start experiencing the results, you will not feel like stopping with the diet and will continue with it for a lifetime.

All the best!

The end... almost!

Reviews are not easy to come by.

As an independent author with a tiny marketing budget, I rely on readers, like you, to leave a short review on Amazon.

Even if it's just a sentence or two!

So if you enjoyed the book, please head to the product page, and leave a review as shown below.

I am very appreciative for your review as it truly makes a difference. Thank you from the bottom of my heart for purchasing this book and reading it to the end.